First World War
and Army of Occupation
War Diary
France, Belgium and Germany

30 DIVISION
Divisional Troops
D Squadron 1/1 Lancashire Hussars
9 November 1915 - 30 April 1916

WO95/2321/1

The Naval & Military Press Ltd
www.nmarchive.com
Published in association with The National Archives

Published by

The Naval & Military Press Ltd

Unit 10 Ridgewood Industrial Park,

Uckfield, East Sussex,

TN22 5QE England

Tel: +44 (0) 1825 749494

www.naval-military-press.com

www.nmarchive.com

This diary has been reprinted in facsimile from the original. Any imperfections are inevitably reproduced and the quality may fall short of modern type and cartographic standards.

© **Crown Copyright**
Images reproduced by permission of The National Archives, London, England, 2015.

Contents

Document type	Place/Title	Date From	Date To
Heading	30th Division Divl Artillery 148th Bde R.F.A. Nov 1915-Feb 1919		
Heading	WO95/2321/1 1915 Nov-1916 Apr "D" Squadron 1/1 Lanc Hus		
Heading	30th Division Divl Troops 'D' Sqdn Lancs Hussar Nov 1915-Apr 1916 To 8 Corps		
Heading	30th Division Bde Lancs Hussars Vol I Nov 15 Apr 16		
War Diary	S.S. Pancras	09/11/1915	09/11/1915
War Diary	Harvre	10/11/1915	10/11/1915
War Diary	Villers-Sous-Ailly	11/11/1915	17/11/1915
War Diary	Olin Court Chateau	18/11/1915	27/11/1915
War Diary	Gorges	28/11/1915	30/11/1915
Heading	30th Div 'D' Sq. Lancs. Hussars. Vol. 2		
War Diary	Gorges	01/12/1915	31/12/1915
Heading	D Sqn 1/1 Lancashire Hussars. 30th Div. Cavalry. Volume II. December 1915		
Heading	D Sqn. Lancs. Hussars Vol. 3 Jan 30		
War Diary	Gorges	01/01/1916	08/01/1916
War Diary	Talmas	09/01/1916	09/01/1916
War Diary	La Houssoye	10/01/1916	10/01/1916
War Diary	Chipilly	11/01/1916	30/01/1916
Heading	War Diary Volume III January 1916 "D" Squadron 1/1 Lancs Hussars. 30th Division Cavalry Squadron.		
Heading	To "D" Sq. Lancs Hussars Vol. 4		
War Diary	Chipilly	01/02/1916	29/02/1916
Heading	D Squad Lane Hussars Vol 5 30th Div		
War Diary	Chipilly	01/03/1916	13/03/1916
War Diary	Corbie	14/03/1916	14/03/1916
War Diary	Fremont	15/03/1916	28/03/1916
War Diary	Breilly Chateau	29/03/1916	31/03/1916
Heading	War Diary D Squadron 1/1 Lancs Hussars 30th Div. Cavalry Squadron.		
War Diary	Breilly Chateau	01/04/1916	11/04/1916
War Diary	Hangest	12/04/1916	12/04/1916
War Diary	Framicourt	13/04/1916	25/04/1916
War Diary	Hangest-Sur Somme	26/04/1916	26/04/1916
War Diary	Breilly Chateau	27/04/1916	30/04/1916
Heading	War Diary D. Sqn. 1/1 Lancs Hussars 30th Div. Cav. Sqn.		

30TH DIVISION
DIVL ARTILLERY

148TH BDE R.F.A.
NOV ~~DEC~~ 1915-FEB 1919

WO 95
2321/1

1915 Nov – 1916 Apr
"D" Squadron 1/1 Lanc Hus

30TH DIVISION
DIVL TROOPS

'D' SQDN LANCS HUSSARS
NOV 1915 - APR 1916

To 8 Corps

"Sp: Lauri Stevens"
vol I

121/7634

30th November

Nov. 15.
Apr 16

WAR DIARY or INTELLIGENCE SUMMARY

Army Form C. 2118.

"B" Squadron
1/1 Denes/Hussars 30th Sub. Cavalry

Ref Maps 1/50000 Sheets ANIEN

Hour, Date, Place	Summary of Events and Information	Remarks and references to Appendices
6 pm November 9th/15 S.S. Pancras	Squadron left Amesbury Station in two trains ① 11.40 AM under Capt. RAWSTORNE ② 1.0 PM under Major BROMILOW } for SOUTHAMPTON Embarked at SOUTHAMPTON & sailed at 5.30 PM Meteorological rained hard all day.	Owing to decision of intention there been 2 gun entries lately the R.E. & Denes Hussars men were put on board ship the led to some confusion on this embarking —
7.30 PM November 10th HARVRE	Landed at HARVRE at 11.0 AM. Entrained at Pontde Marchaux left HARVRE at 9.30 PM Meteorological Blowing hard — with Showers of sleet on the night of 9/10th November	No horses damaged in the crossing of the Channel No sign of submarines
7.0 PM November 11th VILLERS-SOUS-AILLY	Detrained at PONT-REMY, after travelling all night at 9.30 AM. marched 5 miles — arrived VILLERS-SOUS-AILLY 1. P.M. Billets f/t men in farms in the village — plenty of straw available — farms very dirty. — troops rather scattered owing to small amount of accommodation in each billet Horses picketed out in an orchard Meteorological Cold & heavy Showers.	
7.0 PM November 12 th VILLERS-SOUS-AILLY	Carried on with Training operations Meteorological rained all day.	

WAR DIARY
or
INTELLIGENCE SUMMARY

(Erase heading not required.)

Army Form C. 2118.

Sqdn M Service Hussars
Lt Col E Cawston

Instructions regarding War Diaries and Intelligence Summaries are contained in F.S. Regs., Part II. and the Staff Manual respectively. Title pages will be prepared in manuscript.

Hour, Date, Place	Summary of Events and Information	Remarks and references to Appendices
7.0 PM November 13th VILLERS-SOUS-AILLY	Continued training of men. Meteorological. Heavy squalls & rain.	
7.0 PM November 14th VILLERS-SOUS-AILLY	Meteorological. Fine day.	
7.0 PM November 15th VILLERS-SOUS-AILLY	Wire received from headquarters 30th Division that Division would move from present area of concentration to FLESSELLES on Wednesday night of 14/15th November. Meteorological. Slight fall of snow during early part of morning. Soon thawed.	
7.0 PM November 16th VILLERS-SOUS-AILLY	Operation orders received from the headquarters 30th Division for move of Division to FLESSELLES & allotment to areas on arrival there. Lance Hussars reduced to move on 18th. Meteorological. 3"or 4" snow fell during night 15/16 November. Thawed during the day but to began to freeze during evening.	
7.0 PM November 17th VILLERS-SOUS-AILLY	Meteorological. Thawed during day but frozen rain in forenoon. Wet night 17/18.	
7.0 PM November 18th to OLINCOURT CHATEAU	March from VILLERS-SOUS-AILLY to OLINCOURT CHATEAU via FLIXECOURT & VIGNACOURT with 30th Division, advance guard of Yeomanry. Passed billeting parties at 4 P.M. Billets in farm buildings & huts on the ground by regiments. 12 noon arrived OLINCOURT CHATEAU. Ground very bad as had advanced. No fires. Meteorological. Frost early. Rain as day advanced. No fires.	Conditions of roads bad. Transport though stuck with posts kept harness repaired in steam Mills did not arrive till about 7 hours late. Squadrons billeted in farm buildings held on the ground by regiments. Mackintoshes Unstable of Place of Squadrons on the ground considerably restricted by wire.

1247 W.3299 200,000 (E) 8/14 J.B.C. & A. Forms/C. 2118/11.

WAR DIARY
or
INTELLIGENCE SUMMARY

Army Form C. 2118.

(Erase heading not required.)

Instructions regarding War Diaries and Intelligence Summaries are contained in F. S. Regs., Part II. and the Staff Manual respectively. Title pages will be prepared in manuscript.

"A" Sqn. 1/1 Northumberland Hussars
3rd Brig. Cavalry.

Hour, Date, Place	Summary of Events and Information	Remarks and references to Appendices
7.0 PM November 19th OLINCOURT CHATEAU	Meteorological. Cold NE wind, bright sun	
7.0 PM November 20th OLINCOURT CHATEAU	Meteorological. Cold NE wind + dull — some frost during night 25 pm	
7.0 PM November 21st OLINCOURT CHATEAU	Meteorological. Cold NE wind + dull.	
7.0 PM November 22nd OLINCOURT CHATEAU	Meteorological. v. Foggy.	
7.0 PM November 23rd OLINCOURT CHATEAU	Meteorological. Foggy.	
7.0 PM November 24th OLINCOURT CHATEAU	Meteorological. Fine bright frosty day	
7.0 PM November 25th OLINCOURT CHATEAU	Meteorological. do	
7.0 PM November 26th OLINCOURT CHATEAU	Meteorological. do	
7.0 PM November 27th OLINCOURT CHATEAU	Orders received on assumption of Division into first Army of Squadron to proceed to GORGES also march orders for Troop.	
7.0 PM November 27th OLINCOURT CHATEAU	Meteorological. Fine bright cold — freezing slightly all day. March 2 riding horses + one light Draught to accompany to mobile Vet Section — Remainder Squadron Hussars head of Column to march from cross roads N of OLINCOURT CHATEAU at 9.30 AM via HAVERNAS-CH- CANAPES to march arrive GORGES 11.45 AM distance approximately 10 miles — Routes good —	Billets all horses under cover for first time, in Transvaal stables. Men accommodated in Barns Horses + men of each Troop concentrated. Make march from for Remounts drawn from 1 mule away.
7.0 PM November 28th GORGES	Meteorological. Bright but cold — Freezing all day.	2 Wells without from which water drawn.

1247 W 3299 200,000 (E) 8/14 J.B.C. & A. Forms/C. 2118/11.

Army Form C. 2118.

B Sqn 1/1 Lanc. Hussars
30th Brit. Cavalry

WAR DIARY
or
INTELLIGENCE SUMMARY
(Erase heading not required.)

Instructions regarding War Diaries and Intelligence Summaries are contained in F. S. Regs., Part II. and the Staff Manual respectively. Title pages will be prepared in manuscript.

Hour, Date, Place	Summary of Events and Information	Remarks and references to Appendices
7.0 PM 29th November /15 GORGES	Meteorological. Clear & windy morning — rained hard pm all day	
3.0 PM 30th November GORGES	Meteorological. Much warmer, fine still, becoming duller as day advanced. Reconnaissance. A road reconnaissance made to be made by G.S. of 30th Division of Divisional Billeting area — HEM - OUTREBOIS - LE MAILLARD - PROUVILLE - RIBEAUCOURT - ST HILAIRE - ST. LEGER - ST OUEN - CANAPLES - BONNEVILLE - CANDAS - LONGUEVILLETTE - HEM + roads leading out of the area to the DOULLENS - TALMAS road & the line TALMAS - HAVERNAS — Aux. Cyclists allotted all roads N of & including the road DOMART - BERNEUIL - FIENVILLERS - CANDAS - VERT GALAND P.G. Div. Cavalry all roads south of above. J.M.

1247 W 3299 200,000 (E) 8/14 J.B.C. & A. Forms/C. 2118/11.

"Dr. H. Lewis Hussars
Vol: 2

131.
───
7936

30/h/[?]

Army Form C. 2118.

WAR DIARY
or
INTELLIGENCE SUMMARY
(Erase heading not required.)

Account Vol. II

"B" Squadron
1/ Lancashire Hussars
35th Divisional Cavalry

Instructions regarding War Diaries and Intelligence Summaries are contained in F. S. Regs, Part II. and the Staff Manual respectively. Title pages will be prepared in manuscript.

Hour, Date, Place	Summary of Events and Information	Remarks and references to Appendices
7.0 PM Dec 1/1915 GORGES	Meteorological rained most of the day	Health of Men Certain number of men of Squadron admitted to rest muggy weather
7.0 PM Dec 2nd/1915 GORGES	Meteorological rained most of the day 46 Remounts arrived at DOULLENS for the Division	Boots Boots issued to one of Lieut. as special of our Squadron beginning to show trouble after Signe of wear — this Horses appear to be much inclined to readily as the men have down to better themselves to work.
7.0 PM Dec 3rd/1915 GORGES	Meteorological very wet all day Remounts brought to various by Lancashire Hussars were distributed to Units	
7.0 PM Dec 4/1915 GORGES	Meteorological Showery much warmer	
7.0 PM Dec 5th/1915 GORGES	Meteorological Showers — very warm	
7.0 PM Dec 6th/1915 GORGES	Meteorological Showery warm	
7.0 PM Dec 7th/1915 GORGES	Meteorological Raining nearly all day	
7.0 PM Dec 8th/1915 GORGES	Meteorological Showery warm	
7.0 PM Dec 9th/1915 GORGES	Meteorological Wet all day warm	
7.0 PM Dec 10th/1915 GORGES	Meteorological Showery in morning fine afternoon warm	

WAR DIARY or INTELLIGENCE SUMMARY

Army Form C. 2118.

D.S. Meadow
1/1 Leic Hussars

(Erase heading not required.)

Hour, Date, Place	Summary of Events and Information	Remarks and references to Appendices
7.0 PM Dec 11th 1915 GORGES	Antiaircraft Showing in morning fine in afternoon Cooler	Von Stenbock (1) In improvements + elaborating huns from tese tomes = establish on new latrine + new cookhouse (2) Typering of men in trop reading, to attending crossroads + intercommunication Horses Noticed to be losing condition slightly — This attributed (1) to heavy Cooks + Bullies from new Chiefourg — no Chopping machine being provided (2) lack of Closp to more used bee corn. Training Continued Intercommunication Schemes of a similar pattern used from usual Cyclists
7.0 PM Dec 12th 1915 GORGES	Meteorological Some showers — some frost overnight 12/13	
7.0 PM Dec 13th 1915 GORGES	Meteorological Much Colder frire tonight — signs of frost	
7.0 PM Dec 14th 1915 GORGES	Meteorological Showery	
7.0 PM Dec 15th 1915 GORGES	Meteorological Showery	
7.0 PM Dec 16th 1915 GORGES	Meteorological Showery	
7.0 PM Dec 17th 1915 GORGES & 18th 1915 GORGES	Meteorological Fair in morning very wet in afternoon Meteorological Fine — no rain Operation order no 5 issued that 21st Brigade from division a cover that 30 am place would be taken by 21st Brigade from the Division March to attached for [illeg] on 10th & 22 instant	
7.0 PM Dec 19th 1915 GORGES	Meteorological Fine & bright	
7.0 PM Dec 20th 1915 GORGES	Meteorological fine abright in afternoon clearing appearance of frost	
7.0 PM Dec 21st 1915 GORGES	Meteorological Very wet all day	

Army Form C. 2118.

WAR DIARY
or
INTELLIGENCE SUMMARY
(Erase heading not required.)

"D" Squadron
1/1 Lincs Hussars

Instructions regarding War Diaries and Intelligence Summaries are contained in F. S. Regs., Part II. and the Staff Manual respectively. Title pages will be prepared in manuscript.

Hour, Date, Place	Summary of Events and Information	Remarks and references to Appendices
7.0 PM December 22nd 1915 GORGES	Meteorological. Wet all day	Grenadiers. The GOC of Division having decided that all ranks of Brit Cavalry should be trained in use of hand grenades for the purpose of supplying Bombing Parties if necessary. Training in this branch was commenced on December 27th.
7.0 PM December 23rd 1915 GORGES	Meteorological. Wet all day – fine intervals in afternoon	
7.0 PM December 24th 1915 GORGES.	Meteorological. A great deal of rain overnight 23/24th. Heavy showers	
7.0 PM December 25th 1915 GORGES	Meteorological. Very heavy showers. Fine intervals warm	
7.0 PM December 26th 1915 GORGES	Meteorological. Some showers warm	Move. In operation Order No 6 received on December 29th as to move of 30th Division into ST QUENTIN area ETINEHEM to take over this line. March orders commencing 2nd & 8th January for all formations & units except 1st Cavalry & 2nd Armoured Artillery receipt.
7.0 PM December 27th 1915 GORGES	Meteorological. Fine but dull warm	
7.0 PM December 28th 1915 GORGES	Meteorological. Fine & bright warm	
7.0 PM December 29th 1915 GORGES.	Meteorological. Fine morning turning to rain later	
7.0 PM December 30th 1915 GORGES	Meteorological. & stormy colder	
12.0 Noon December 31st 1915 GORGES	Meteorological. Fine heavy rain overnight	Draft – Horses. 1 C – 1 R received to replace casualty on December 29th. Health of Men very little sickness.

J.H. Crombleholme Major
O.C. "D" Sqn 1/1 Lincs Hussars
30th Div. Cavalry.

Army Form C. 2118.

WAR DIARY
of
SUMMARY OF EVENTS AND INFORMATION

Sqn 1/1 Lancashire Hussars.
30th A.T. Cavalry

Volume II

December 1915.

"D" Sp: Lanes: Aursan
Vol: 3

Army Form C. 2118.

WAR DIARY
or
INTELLIGENCE SUMMARY
(Erase heading not required.)

Volume III January 1916. A Sqn
 1/1 Lancs Hussars 30th Div: Cavalry

Instructions regarding War Diaries and Intelligence Summaries are contained in F. S. Regs., Part II. and the Staff Manual respectively. Title pages will be prepared in manuscript.

Hour, Date, Place	Summary of Events and Information	Remarks and references to Appendices
7.0 PM January 1st 1916 GORGES	Meteorological. Fine morning turned to rain later. Warm.	Horses Six horses at GORGES being
7.0 PM Jan. 2nd 1916 GORGES	Meteorological. Fine & bright	which have the horse-men who have over but 6 some
7.0 PM Jan. 3rd 1916 GORGES	Meteorological. Steady drizzle all day. Orders: Addendum to Operation Order No 6 received + march table for Arl: Cavalry, Field Ambulances + Divisional Artillery.	considerable improvement in horses condition
7.0 PM Jan. 4th 1916 GORGES.	Meteorological. Showers.	All horses been watched to be clipped have high keep it hard to be done with
7.0 PM Jan. 5th 1916 GORGES	Meteorological. Fine morning. Some rain later	hand clippers – this fact prevents the large amount
7.0 PM Jan. 6th 1916 GORGES	Meteorological. Some rain – rather windy	of condition then lost in horses through sweating
7.0 PM Jan. 7th 1916 GORGES	Meteorological. Bright cold early, turning to rain + wind later.	etc
7.0 PM Jan. 8th 1916 GORGES	Meteorological. Rain all day.	
7.0 PM Jany 9th 1916 GORGES TALMAS	Meteorological. Fine & bright. Colder. March Commenced into 5th Divisional area. 6/7 GORGES 11.0 AM arrived TALMAS 2.15PM distance about 10 miles. A little footsoreness in spite of number of troops having to march through water masses. Horses under cover	

Volume III

Army Form C. 2118.

WAR DIARY
or
INTELLIGENCE SUMMARY
(Erase heading not required.)

A S Wadsworth
1/1 Lance Hussars 30th Divisional Cavalry

Hour, Date, Place	Summary of Events and Information	Remarks and references to Appendices
7.0 PM January 10th 1916 LA HOUSSOYE	Meteorological Same drizzle all day. 2nd day of march into 5th Divisional area. Distance approx. 14 miles. Regt TALMAS 9.45 AM arrived LA HOUSSOYE 2.0 PM. Halt 1/2 hour midway fed at QUERRIEU where there is a good stream for watering horses. Billets very fair — moderately clean. Horses under cover. Clean billets had been made ready for all Regts of 30th Division marching through to its area down billets en route. Stores.	Transport. Baggage & Supply waggons left first line in its separate rear small column on 1st. — Owing to slow rate of march the transport was close to column all the time. One extra waggon to War establishment allowed for baggage which was extra baggage —— Men have room —— men have canned rollen on top. Icelaine Mintoss. HTF
7.0 PM January 11th 1916 CHIPILLY	Meteorological Same slight rain. Running to drizzle towards evening. Reg't TALMAS 9.45 AM arrived CHIPILLY 2.0 PM. Distance approx 6 miles. Billets owing to amount of accommodation & amount of troops coming into the village it took a considerable time to fit horses & men into billets & the Squadron was somewhat mixed up with other units in the Division. Horses here all out on our night of 11/1/16 January, the pleasing rain 12 & horse standing with out under cover in open stalls. 3rd troops picketted in a small avenue. Subsequently got under cover in cart sheds. HTF

WAR DIARY or INTELLIGENCE SUMMARY

Army Form C. 2118.

Volume VII

Instructions regarding War Diaries and Intelligence Summaries are contained in F.S. Regs., Part II. and the Staff Manual respectively. Title pages will be prepared in manuscript.

B S Gladrow 1/1 Shrops Hussars
30th Divisional Cavalry

(Erase heading not required.)

Hour, Date, Place	Summary of Events and Information	Remarks and references to Appendices
7.0 PM January 12th 1916 CHIPILLY	Meteorological. Drizzling rain all day.	Detached P.o.C. 1 Sgt, 1 Cpl, 12 men sent to A.P.M. to be trained in استعمال regulation of traffic.
7.0 PM January 13th 1916 CHIPILLY	Meteorological. Bright cold – Squalls of snow later in afternoon.	1 Officer + 15 NCOs having finished course of duties of the A.P.M. returned to the regulation of the traffic during a battle.
7.0 PM January 14th 1916 CHIPILLY	Meteorological. Bright cold – Country drying up.	Detached for Gunnedah Park. 1 Sgt + 1 private + go to the XIIIth Corps to form portion of an observation post in conjunction with an officer + 3 men from Divisional Cyclists.
7.0 PM January 15th 1916 CHIPILLY	Meteorological. Fine most of day, occasional drizzling rain.	Fatigue Parties
7.0 PM January 16th 1916 CHIPILLY	Meteorological. Fine bright mild.	engaged on constructing wash for the erection of horse shelters for 3 + 4 troops
7.0 PM January 17th 1916 CHIPILLY	Meteorological. Dull no rain – colder	also parties engaged on
7.0 PM January 18th 1916 CHIPILLY	Meteorological. Dull rain most of day.	pulling down horse standing to which stone procured from a fallen down cottage adjacent
7.0 PM January 19th 1916 CHIPILLY	Meteorological. Fine several hours sunshine.	
7.0 PM January 20th 1916 CHIPILLY	Meteorological. Fine – Several hours sunshine	
7.0 PM January 21st 1916 CHIPILLY	Meteorological. Fine but dull rather windy	

Volume III   Army Form C. 2118.
                                    "B" Squadron
                                    1/1 Lincs Hussars
                                    30th A.W.L. Cavalry

WAR DIARY
or
INTELLIGENCE SUMMARY
(Erase heading not required.)

Instructions regarding War Diaries and Intelligence
Summaries are contained in F.S. Regs., Part II.
and the Staff Manual respectively. Title pages
will be prepared in manuscript.

Hour, Date, Place	Summary of Events and Information	Remarks and references to Appendices
7.0 PM January 22nd 1916 CHIPILLY	Meteorological dull, occasional showers.	Forage Horses Amount of hay allowance down from 12lbs to 6lbs from January 11th
7.0 PM January 23rd 1916 CHIPILLY	Meteorological - Snow - mild	
7.0 PM January 24th 1916 CHIPILLY	Meteorological Snow - mild	
7.0 PM January 25th 1916 CHIPILLY	Meteorological Snow - mild	
7.0 PM January 26th 1916 CHIPILLY	Meteorological Snow occasional showers.	
7.0 PM January 27th 1916 CHIPILLY	Meteorological Snow most day, mild	
7.0 PM January 28th 1916 CHIPILLY	Meteorological Snow most day & in evening - mild. Operation Message from G.S. 30th Division sent off 11:45AM received 12:40PM That squadron was to "Stand to" - Horses kept saddled. Horses saddled up & meet part or squadron G - all ranks slept in boots with ammunition handy, all night. Considerable artillery activity heard in direction of SUZANNE + FROISY in afternoon & during night of 28/29th. Message received on telephone at 8:15PM that Germans had broken through French near FRISE on a front of 500 yds. from Bvil H.Qs.	

Volume III

WAR DIARY
or
INTELLIGENCE SUMMARY
(Erase heading not required.)

Army Form C. 2118.

Instructions regarding War Diaries and Intelligence Summaries are contained in F. S. Regs., Part II. and the Staff Manual respectively. Title pages will be prepared in manuscript.

Hour, Date, Place	Summary of Events and Information	Remarks and references to Appendices
7.0 PM January 29th 1915 CHIPILLY	Meteorological. Misty early, fine interval - country drying up. S Squadron "Standing to all day." No further orders received. Rumours as to what was happening brought in by various soldiers passing through. Considerable numbers of wounded estimated to be coming in to 97th S.H. from BRAY & SUZANNE. Saddles stayed on for a short periods at stables & 2 hours in afternoon as some horses showing signs of girth galls. Continuous artillery firing heard all day without cessation at times very heavy in direction of FRISE which gunners were rumoured to have taken. Orders received at 9.0 PM that men to sleep in boots & puttees. JHA	Instructions received from GOC 30th on Jan 29th that GOC visited all men of S squadron to have 48 hours experience of Fr. trenches. That arrangements to be made with 30th Inf Bde. These arrangements were left up to by the German attack. Forage Dump. March from FROISY to CHIPILLY as in had been settled out of formerplace on 29th. Called out to form escort party. On 30th & 31st. JHA
7.0 PM January 30th 1915 CHIPILLY	Meteorological. Misty early, fine colder. S Squadron still standing to - Lieut Attley fining a search of the men who had been on MMP duty at SUZANNE brought in his horse with nasty shrapnel wound in free by his groom which had been unable to be dressed for 2 days - other groom sent to MVS - This man returned less to had been in SUZANNE while it was heavily shelled & that 6 other men after Squadron who had on orderly duty to Bde HQs + MMP. Were also there. That though village was reduced to ten grooms & everyone escaping have had felt it more Cu him. Two men dispatched for a report to C.C.S at CORBIE. Received from HQs that men again to sleep in boots, puttees. JHA	

WAR DIARY
or
INTELLIGENCE SUMMARY

(Erase heading not required.)

Army Form C. 2118.

Volume III

Instructions regarding War Diaries and Intelligence Summaries are contained in F.S. Regs., Part II. and the Staff Manual respectively. Title pages will be prepared in manuscript.

Hour, Date, Place	Summary of Events and Information	Remarks and references to Appendices
7.0 P.M. January 1915 CHIPILLY	Meteorological. Mostly very fine rather cold. Squadron still "standing by" but fatigues provided as asked. Rumour that the French were hanging up some big guns in order to shell the Germans out of the S. of FRISE, had taken first S. of FRISE. Very heavy artillery firing was heard all afternoon & evening in the direction of FRISE. Message received 9.15 P.M. Sent off from Bn HQrs 7.38 P.M. but "state of readiness to be maintained" & continue during to-night "situation". All ranks slept with clothes on & saddles kept ready. Which horse nosebag + hayg nets filled.	Fatigues. The number of men fatigues which the Squadron called on to perform is greatly leave insufficient men for proper care & exercise of horses. Drafts 1 O.R. arrived Jan 30th to replace 1 man wounded sick Decr 8th 1915. Health of Men. During month of January was good very little sickness. Some men laid up for a few days with children going to be continually in the wet. Horses Good — only one case of prize unsoundness necessary. J.A.A Tomlinson major O.C. A. S Squadron 1/1 Lancs Hussars 30th Divl Cavalry Squadron.

Army Form C.2118

WAR DIARY
INTELLIGENCE SUMMARY
(Erase heading not required)

War Diary
Volume III January 1916.

"D" Squadron
1/1 Lancs Hussars.

30th Division Cavalry Squadron

30. Dʳ Sp: Lancs: Hunan

Vol: 4

Army Form C. 2118.

Volume IV

Instructions regarding War Diaries and Intelligence Summaries are contained in F.S. Regs., Part II. and the Staff Manual respectively. Title pages will be prepared in manuscript.

WAR DIARY
or
INTELLIGENCE SUMMARY

(Erase heading not required.)

10 Squadron
1/1 Lancs Hussars
3 oth Divl Cavalry Squadron

Hour, Date, Place	Summary of Events and Information	Remarks and references to Appendices
7.0 PM January 1st 1916 CHIPILLY	Meteorological Fine but cold rather hazy. Quiet day very little commenced to last — a captive balloon with 3 inch colours sent up about 12 noon & remained up all afternoon in direction of ÉCLUSE of CAPPY. An aeroplane seen flying round it afterwards nothing in — Very little firing hard on night 1/2 2nd. The Squadron were all quiet with orders to hold itself in readiness for emergency.	HJC
7.0 PM January 2nd 1916 CHIPILLY	Meteorological Fine — cold rather hazy. Quiet day not much firing heard — Captive balloon again sent up in same direction as yesterday. About 4pm 4 or 5 paper balloons were seen blowing from a South easterly direction one of these came down near CHIPILLY was brought to HQ Arillon — It was come stated about 3 ft high + made of silky paper it had a small frame like a cigar light attached but it had not been lit — a packet of papers been attached they appeared to be extracts from German Socialist papers + spoken of the change of motion in Germany — Action taken Sent up to Brit Headquarters.	HJC
7.0 PM January 3rd 1916 CHIPILLY	Meteorological Fine — cold not so hazy. Quiet day except for guns registering — Balloon not seen up today 9 German captive balloon up about 3PM Eof CAPPY. Staff of 7th horse collected for the Division & distributed MERICOURT.	HJC

WAR DIARY or INTELLIGENCE SUMMARY

Army Form C. 2118.

Volume V

Instructions regarding War Diaries and Intelligence Summaries are contained in F.S. Regs., Part II. and the Staff Manual respectively. Title pages will be prepared in manuscript.

(Erase heading not required.)

Hour, Date, Place	Summary of Events and Information	Remarks and references to Appendices
February 4th 1916 7.0 PM CHIPILLY	Meteorological. Stormy – a good deal of rain especially in morning. Not much firing heard – squadrons still standing to – arrangements there have been made for letting 5 to go up to trenches for instruction 48 hours on having 5/6 casualties as Divisional Commander has orders to keep the squadron at its disposal as strong as possible. HH	
7.0 PM February 5th 1916 7.0 PM CHIPILLY	Meteorological. Fine at night but atmosphere very cloudy. Considerable aeroplane activity. Hostile aircraft – at approx 11.15 a.m. a hostile aeroplane was attacked by one of ours, it was damaged & seen to have apparently planed down in direction of CAPPY. True to have come down just inside French lines beyond CAPPY, reported to have come down just inside French lines beyond SOMME. Four observation balloons were seen up, two in French side, one near ÉCLUSIER & second approx two miles south of it, one between BOIS LES CELESTINS & BOIS GRESSAIRE & the other approx 1½ to 2 miles N.N.W of it. One on English side of SOMME. The other heard beyond registering. Artillery very little firing. No machine gun fire, no tear number of albeits. The Garrison mayor who thinks frequence so to the number of albeits in the village in view of possible bombardment. HH Situation still continued by the squadron.	
7.0 PM February 6/1916 CHIPILLY	Meteorological. Dull rather windy. Quiet day very little firing heard – Observation balloons not up. Part sent out at 4.15 PM to search country for artillery horses which had stampeded from PRAY & shell had in moveth amongst them HH	

Volume IV

WAR DIARY
or
INTELLIGENCE SUMMARY

Army Form C. 2118.

(Erase heading not required.)

Instructions regarding War Diaries and Intelligence Summaries are contained in F. S. Regs., Part II. and the Staff Manual respectively. Title pages will be prepared in manuscript.

Hour, Date, Place	Summary of Events and Information	Remarks and references to Appendices
7.0 PM February 7th 1916. CHIPILLY.	Meteorological. Strong SW wind - Some rain bright afternoon. Officer balloon at MARICOURT obscuring - not much artillery fire was heard. Initls.	
7.0 PM February 8th 1916 CHIPILLY	Meteorological. Bright & fine. Some rain in evening. Artillery firing heavy between 4.30 PM & 5.30 PM. 5 aviators still in disorders do to services. Initls.	
7.0 PM February 9th 1916 CHIPILLY	Meteorological. dull morning, bright afternoon. Strong observation balloon ship. Heavy artillery firing heard from 5.30 to 6.30 PM.	
7.0 PM February 10th 1916 CHIPILLY	Meteorological. frost overnight - bright, SW wind. Gen Artillery firing heard. Initls.	
7.0 PM February 11th 1916 CHIPILLY	Meteorological. Hot cold day - cold wind. Considerable artillery firing heard at times.	
7.0 PM February 12th 1916 CHIPILLY	Meteorological. Hot morning, fine afternoon. Quarters: Staff of 70 horses + mules allotted + distributed / R received as draft. for the Division.	
7.0 PM February 13th 1916 CHIPILLY	Meteorological. Some rain in morning. fine afternoon, warm. Quiet day. Initls.	

Army Form C. 2118.

WAR DIARY
or
INTELLIGENCE SUMMARY
(Erase heading not required.)

Volume IV

Instructions regarding War Diaries and Intelligence Summaries are contained in F. S. Regs., Part II. and the Staff Manual respectively. Title pages will be prepared in manuscript.

Hour, Date, Place	Summary of Events and Information	Remarks and references to Appendices
7.0 PM February 14th 1916 CHIPILLY	Meteorological: Wet morning – finer afternoon. Quiet day.	Fatigues 15 men on fatigue at Divisional Baths in Cerisy. Laundry commenced 11th inst.
7.0 PM February 15th 1916 CHIPILLY	Meteorological: Wet most of the day. Quiet day.	
7.0 PM February 16th 1916 CHIPILLY	Meteorological: heavy rain and wind in morning, finer afternoon. Quiet Day. Operation order No 7 received March Orders on relief of 36th Division by 51st. L.H.Q. to change on relief. N.I.H at Co RAIE on J.U.52.58.	
7.0 PM February 17th 1916 CHIPILLY	Meteorological: Some rain in morning, fine afternoon cold & wind. Quiet Day.	
7.0 PM February 18th 1916 CHIPILLY	Meteorological: Very wet all day. Quiet day. Staff of 48 horse shelters for Division Collectur at MERICOURT. Now received cancelling operation Order No 8 for move.	Horses Draft of 2 horses received to replace ones invalid.
7.0 PM February 19th 1916 CHIPILLY	Meteorological: much rain, fine intervals. Quiet day. Constructive at present finish overnight.	
7.0 PM February 20th 1916 CHIPILLY	Meteorological: fine & bright. Quiet day.	

Volume IV

WAR DIARY
or
INTELLIGENCE SUMMARY

Army Form C. 2118.

(Erase heading not required.)

Hour, Date, Place	Summary of Events and Information	Remarks and references to Appendices
7.0 PM February 21st 1916 CHIPILLY	Meteorological. Bright but cold. NE wind. Dull afternoon. Heavy artillery firing heard S of the SOMME in the French area commencing approx 1.30 AM to 11.0 AM when it gradually subsided — ① No hostile aircraft came over CHIPILLY about 10.0 AM when German fliers fired on but not touched one of them. Went back over the top of Captain balloons at MERICOURT but did not attack it — 2nd one working in northerly direction — Rumour that Germans had made a gas shell & gas attack on French 3 or 4 miles S of the SOMME & had been heavily repulsed — Subsequently confirmed	(TM)
7.0 PM February 22nd 1916 CHIPILLY	Meteorological. Frost in early morning — some snow & sleet in afternoon. Otherwise still. Commenced firing heard about 5.45 PM	
7.0 P.M February 23rd 1916 CHIPILLY	Meteorological. Frost in morning & first [?] Quiet day	Zn B
7.0 P.M February 24th 1916 CHIPILLY	Meteorological. Some rain in night & hard frost all day — very fine. Received 3rd Army Order No G 746 on conduct of Aircraft Guns Brit Sqn L Sqnd to Report 13th Corps now A 3670 cancels all leave Esq HA 18 & enrolments until further notice	
7.0 p.m February 25th 1916 CHIPILLY	Meteorological. Severe most of day & frost all day. About 3" of snow on ground when I ceased snowing about 3 pm. Rumours of enemy success near VERDUN & capture of a considerable amount of French prisoners. Quiet day.	Zn B

Army Form C. 2118.

WAR DIARY
or
INTELLIGENCE SUMMARY
(Erase heading not required.)

Instructions regarding War Diaries and Intelligence Summaries are contained in F. S. Regs., Part II. and the Staff Manual respectively. Title pages will be prepared in manuscript.

Hour, Date, Place	Summary of Events and Information	Remarks and references to Appendices
7-0 p.m. February 26th 1916 CHIPILLY	Meteorological. Had frost during night & in morning, thawed to them about 11 a.m. Quiet day. Collected 39 hours 3 mins. for division at MERICOURT	26/3. Health of men. During month we had – a few cases of influenza, colds rheumatism & pneumonia. One Officer & NCO & 15 men went to CCS Hospital complaints.
7-0 p.m. February 27th 1916 CHIPILLY	Meteorological. Frost in night. Thaw & some rain in morning. Fine afternoon. Collected 7 men & D horses from MERICOURT the night of Feb 26/27th. Quiet day	Horses. Others OR'd etc from trouble. Gravels. One shot with bad foot. A certain number of kicks & lessons. Some B horses show skin trouble which necessitated clipping. One IB was lost after developing diagnosed complaint. T.A.B. The time for soil caused the horses to become v. fickle when being groomed. That
7-0 p.m. February 28th 1916 CHIPILLY	Meteorological. Frost in night. Thaw & some rain in morning. Fine afternoon. Reported that 73 shells were fired into BRAY-SUR-SOMME night of Feb 27/28th. Continuous slow fire apparently on S. side of SOMME began about 2-50 p.m. & continued until about 5-30 p.m. A battalion of Gordon Highlanders with Transport marched through Valley between 4 & 5 p.m. from towards SAILLY LAURETTE – this delay to 51st Div 2nd CL	
7-0 p.m. February 29th 1916 CHIPILLY	Meteorological. Showers. Fine afternoon. Considerable aeroplane activity in morning. Intermittent cannonade all day	

J.A.H. Crombie
Major

D. Saral
Lane Hughes
Vol 5
30 n D 3

Volume

WAR DIARY
or
INTELLIGENCE SUMMARY
(Erase heading not required.)

Army Form C. 2118.

A. S. Squadron
Lance Hussars
302 (Divisional Cavalry) Sqn.

Instructions regarding War Diaries and Intelligence Summaries are contained in F. S. Regs, Part II. and the Staff Manual respectively. Title pages will be prepared in manuscript.

Hour, Date, Place	Summary of Events and Information	Remarks and references to Appendices
7-0 p.m. March 1st 1916 CHIPILLY	Meteorological. Fine day. Very quiet day.	
7.0 PM March 2nd 1916 CHIPILLY	Meteorological. Fine occasional showers. Quiet day.	
7.0 PM March 3rd 1916 CHIPILLY	Meteorological. Fine but dull. Quiet day.	
7.0 PM March 4th 1916 CHIPILLY	Meteorological. Snow fell most of day dull & cold. Quiet day.	
7.0 PM March 5th 1916 CHIPILLY	Meteorological. Fine. Showers overnight. Quiet day.	
7.0 PM March 6th 1916 CHIPILLY	Meteorological. Slight frost. Fine & sunny in morning. Snow storm afternoon. Squadron was inspected by the GOC of the Division. Orders received for Squadron to commence a 14 days Course of Instruction in the Trenches with R.S.F.	
7.0 PM March 7th 1916 CHIPILLY	Meteorological. Sharp frost in morning. Remainder later. Quiet day. 20 men under Lieut. J.N. Slumber start up to start Trench Training - Sector 2 - near SUZANNE (MOULIN FARGNY).	
7.0 PM March 8th 1916 CHIPILLY	Meteorological. Fine & bright. Quiet day.	

Army Form C. 2118.

WAR DIARY
or
INTELLIGENCE SUMMARY
(Erase heading not required.)

D Squadron
11th Lancs Hussars
30th Divisional Cavalry Sqn

Hour, Date, Place	Summary of Events and Information	Remarks and references to Appendices
7.0 PM March 9th 1916 CHIPILLY	Meteorological Fine & Bright, Snow on the night 9/10. Quiet day.	
7.0 PM March 10th 1916 CHIPILLY	Meteorological Snow in morning, dull & cold remainder of day. Quiet day.	
7.0 PM March 11th 1916 CHIPILLY	Meteorological Since dull & cold. Trench Party. 1st Lord Fatlom & D.O.B sent up to relieve Party under Lieut Blundell. Relief to take place at 7.0 P.M. Wire received at 12 midnight that Squadron Lancs Hussars to concentrate at CHIPILLY by evening of 12th in case the proposed to march on 14th — actor ordered.	No Casualties amongst trench Party. Duck post on this night was attacked on night of the relief & then had to stand to for 1½ hours on S.O.S being sent out. No attack was made on ISLAND POST or FARGNY MILL when D B Lun dells Party were on the
7.0 PM March 12th 1916 CHIPILLY	Meteorological Bright & warm. Wire sent to adjutant R.S.F at 9.0 AM that L Lord Fatlom to march Party, not to return - gallop returned at 3.30 PM G CHIPILLY. Owing to deficiencies in Communication trench SUZANNE AVENUE it took them some time to get out. Horses sent up to meet them at CHATEAU SUZANNE. Artillery fairly active on the front. Orderly received from A.A.Q.M.G that Sgt. to find working Party to Heller & Cpl. to act brushed at FRÉMONT	Staff horses. 2 R. received on 12 Front & Cpl. received on 12 Front

WAR DIARY or INTELLIGENCE SUMMARY

Army Form C. 2118.

VOLUMEN

Hour, Date, Place	Summary of Events and Information	Remarks and references to Appendices
7.0 PM March 13th 1916 CHIPILLY	Meteorological Bright warm. Operation order No.11 received — Sqn. to march est. 9.30AM on 14th to CORBIE to bn 15th to FREMONT — acknowledgt. 9.15AM	D.S. qr. M. Farrier Sergeant S/Sgt Bn. Can. Sgt. No.1 Sqns. R.Sharpshooter Sgt. Saddler appointed to from C. Sgt. S/Sgt Nuesfield promoted S.Q.M.S.
7.0 PM March 14th 1916 CORBIE	Meteorological Bright warm Sqn. marched from CHIPILLY 9.30AM arrived CORBIE 12.0 noon distance approx 7½ miles Good Billets for men Horses all under cover in stables.	Transport Supplies in 2 G.S. wagons Baggage one 3 tonner long.
7.0 PM March 15th 1916 FREMONT	Meteorological Bright warm Sqn. marched from CORBIE 8.45AM arrived FREMONT 1.0PM distance approx 14 miles 1st & 2nd Lines transport left to follow on slowly. Motor lorry stuck in mud about 1 mile from FREMONT this necessitated sending horse transport back & transferring baggage. Rations to have been drawn at AILLY-SUR-SOMME dump to have to be motored here, but motor lorry having moved from here been lorry lorries are having march from here to LONGPRÉ 25 KILOS distant — No forage is available hert following day where camion station for military feeds.	Billets FREMONT as the village was marked out for an infantry batt. Plenty of accommodation for men & horses 3 Troops have been Corn No other Troops in village.

WAR DIARY or INTELLIGENCE SUMMARY

Army Form C. 2118.

(Erase heading not required.)

O. Owen
B. Sgr
1/1 Lancs Hussars
30th Divn. Cav. Sqr.

Hour, Date, Place	Summary of Events and Information	Remarks and references to Appendices
7.0 PM March 16th FREMONT	Meteorological Bright morning dull & snow rain in afternoon. Working Party Sent out to TERANCOURT to ar & take knapwood for dumping on canal bank at AILLY-SUR-SOMME for removal to depot. 1 Officer & a platoon of 2nd Battn/Wilts Regt arrived for attachment for a working party. Patrols arrangements made for drawing further rations. Cavalrie enclosed as a dump is as established at LONGPRÉ. Patrols at 4 Cross roads between VAUX & VAST to return details of 49th Division left behind & who was within 2 miles of FREMONT & around a considerable journey.	Working Parties Taking over from 18th Division — come under orders of C.E. XIII Corps. Particulars Loading knapwood PERTANGES STN & MERICOURT for rail. Loading snow limbs onto rail at VIGNACOURT. Cutting 6'x 6' pickets at TERANCOURT from willows. Conveying to dump at AILLY-SUR-SOMME. 5 motor lorries attached for this work. HAT
7.0 PM March 17th FREMONT	Meteorological Fine & Bright	
7.0 PM March 18th FREMONT	Meteorological Fine	
7.0 PM March 19th FREMONT	Meteorological Fine & Sunny	
7.0 PM March 20th FREMONT	Meteorological Fine	HAT

Army Form C. 2118.

WAR DIARY
or
INTELLIGENCE SUMMARY
(Erase heading not required.)

Instructions regarding War Diaries and Intelligence Summaries are contained in F.S. Regs, Part II. and the Staff Manual respectively. Title pages will be prepared in manuscript.

Volume N

NSgn
Prince Hussars
3rd Brit Cavalry Bgr.

Hour, Date, Place	Summary of Events and Information	Remarks and references to Appendices
7.0 PM March 21st FREMONT	Meteorological Fine	Billets FREMONT Very good - all farms had been prepared with trunks for men. Horses have all under cover
7.0 PM March 22nd FREMONT	Meteorological Fine	
7.0 PM March 23rd FREMONT	Meteorological Snow most of day	
7.0 PM March 24th FREMONT	Meteorological Cold + Somewhat	
7.0 PM March 25th FREMONT	Meteorological Frost in morning Fine	
7.0 PM March 26th FREMONT	Meteorological Something in morning Otherwise bright afternoon	
7.0 PM March 27th FREMONT	Meteorological Bright in morning Cold wind Much afternoon. Operation NO 12 received — 30th Division to move back into an area W of AMIENS - DOULLENS road (less hackery parties + divisional Schools). Orders issued to move from FREMONT to AILLY-SUR-SOMME on 29/3. Acknowledge.	
7.0 PM March 28th FREMONT	Meteorological Fine - very cold wind. Billeting Officer sent on to make arrangement (and throw any accommodation at AILLY-SUR-SOMME — Referred to AA + QMG — Now received at 6.30 PM letter & Division to proceed to BERTANGLES on 29/3.	

WAR DIARY or INTELLIGENCE SUMMARY

Army Form C. 2118.

Hour, Date, Place	Summary of Events and Information	Remarks and references to Appendices
PM March 29th 1916 BREILLY CHATEAU	Meteorological. Sunny with cold wind. Some snow. Staff officer & flying Corps informed O.C. Sqn. at 8:30am in morning that no billeting accommodation at BERTANGLES = Billets other than BREILLY. Sent Galloper to report this — Message received 11:45am that Squadron to proceed to BREILLY CHATEAU to billet. Squadron marched from FREMONT 12:15 PM arrived BREILLY 2:00 PM. Watered horses en route at AILLY-SUR-SOMME. Distance about 6 miles.	BREILLY CHATEAU: Good — troops accommodated in a large loft. All horses together in large stables attached to farm.
PM March 30th 1916 BREILLY CHATEAU	Meteorological. Post early — Sunny storm. Troop drill training — musketry & sword exercise & signalling.	Hotchkiss gun having been sent for instructional purposes. Training commenced in same.
PM March 31st 1916 BREILLY CHATEAU	Meteorological. Slung storm. Troop training — musketry. Programme of training up to April 8th sent in to G. Staff includes some combined training with cyclists & motor machine gun battery.	Horse Equitation 4 O.R. sat down H.Q.S. to Base for discharge during month. Draft. 2 O.R. arrived demo month. 3 Horses arrived at FREMONT. H.A.A. rounds maps O.C. N. Sqn. travel to Dampes BDBBnCavSqn 4 N. Sqn travel BDBBnCavSqn

A Sqn. N. Farce Hussars BDBBn Cav Sqn

War Diary
A Squadron
11th Lancer Hussars
3rd (Br)(?) Cavalry Squadron

Army Form C. 2118

VOL. 6

WAR DIARY
or
INTELLIGENCE SUMMARY

(Erase heading not required.)

Volume VI

Hour, Date, Place	Summary of Events and Information	Remarks and references to Appendices
7.0 PM April 1st 1916 BREILLY CHATEAU	Meteorological bright sunshine warm Training	
7.0 PM April 2nd 1916 BREILLY CHATEAU	Meteorological troop & squadron drill afternoon much & Shorley exercise bright sunshine warm	
7.0 PM April 3rd 1916 BREILLY CHATEAU	Meteorological bright sunshine warm Training continued as above	
7.0 PM April 4th 1916 BREILLY CHATEAU	Meteorological colder, dull all day some rain in evening Training continued	
7.0 PM April 5th 1916 BREILLY CHATEAU	Meteorological fine bright morning dull afternoon Training — tactical scheme with cyclists + machine gun battery. Letter received from G.S. that 8 m + cyclists to proceed on 12th for 14 days training attachment to Anzac Div. Indian Cavalry Division at FRANCOURT	10R evacuated to C.C.S
7.0 PM April 6th 1916 BREILLY CHATEAU	Meteorological fine rather dull. Training continued	
7.0 PM April 7th 1916 BREILLY CHATEAU	Meteorological fine bright warm Training continued	HAS

Army Form C. 2118.

WAR DIARY
or
INTELLIGENCE SUMMARY
(Erase heading not required.)

B Squadron
1/1 Lancs. Hussars.

Volume VI

Hour, Date, Place	Summary of Events and Information	Remarks and references to Appendices
April 8th 1916 7.0 PM BREILLY CHATEAU	Meteorological Strict alright - warm Training contd.	
April 9th 1916 7.0 PM BREILLY CHATEAU	Meteorological Fine, bright, warm	
April 10th 1916 7.0 PM BREILLY CHATEAU	Meteorological Dull all day - colder. Training contd. M.O. reported Squadron prior to proceeding for isolation to AMBALA BDE	Draft 1 Cpl + 2 men arrive No 5 General B.D. at HAVRE were some time exposed to men ones to base for training.
April 11th 1916 7.0 PM BREILLY CHATEAU	Meteorological Some rain in morning dull later Training contd. 2 Men from XIIIth Corps Observation Post - also 2 men attached to 2nd Sqn RFC 28 grooms & 3 horses reported to Sqn.	Draft 2 "R" horses arrival
April 12th 1916 7.0 PM HANGEST	Meteorological Very hot Sqn. commenced march to FRAMICOURT for training under Ambala Cav. Bde Marching out state :- officers 5 ; OR 129 + ASC Horses 144 + 8 104 + 5 transport horses; Sick Hospital: 3 in; 2 attached to Brit. School 1 am MVS AM Dep. 10:30 arr. 4.0 pm. Village empty of troops. Ample Billets for men Horses all under cover.	Transport 1 extra GS wagon allowed. 1st line transport accompanied Squadron and 2nd line remained. kept for base wte.
April 13th 1916 7.0 PM FRAMICOURT	Meteorological Windy, bright intervals Issued Operation orders 3 Heads of columns to pass church at Flixecourt lines attached to Sqn. march to march to ck at 8.40 AM Sqn. dep. 9.0 AM Sahn. to Lights Car 8.50 AM arr. 3.0 PM 10 mm'a Battery Car. Sqn 9.0 AM Distance approx 23 miles midday halt at WOIREL	Billets Fair - Considerable difficulty in getting field for horses - eventually reasonable accommodation from farmer attended under orders from Brigadier H.Q. HAS

Forms/C. 2118/11.

WAR DIARY
or
INTELLIGENCE SUMMARY

(Erase heading not required.)

Army Form C. 2118.

Volume VI

A.S. anderson
4 Services Hussars
30th Brit. Cav. Sqn.

Hour, Date, Place	Summary of Events and Information	Remarks and references to Appendices
P.M. 7.0 April 14th 1916 FRAMICOURT	Meteorological. Wind, rain, heavy rain on night 13/13. Training under Programme issued by AMBALA CAV. BDE. Sqn. only Patrolling & despatch riding. Order received from 30th Brit. Division that all men on leave except special leave be stopped by 18th. More Sqn. officers.	
P.M. 7.0 April 15th 1916 FRAMICOURT	Meteorological. Cold – heavy showers of hail & sleet in morning. Parade cancelled by Bde. Hqrs.	
P.M. 7.0 April 16th 1916 FRAMICOURT	Meteorological. Fine & bright. Sqn. training. Indian servant for A/Major Twists, late Staff of AMBALA Cavalry Brigade.	
P.M. 7.0 April 17th 1916 FRAMICOURT	Meteorological. Some rain early. Fine later. Tactical Exercise of Brit. M.I. Troops & M.G. battery under the Staff of AMBALA Cavalry Bde.	
P.M. 7.0 April 18th 1916 FRAMICOURT	Meteorological. Hot all day. Strong S.W. wind. Parade cancelled.	
P.M. 7.0 April 19th 1916 FRAMICOURT	Meteorological. Hot most of day. Strong S.A. wind. Parade cancelled.	Draft I.O.R. arrived from Base was discharged. HAD
P.M. 7.0 April 20th 1916 FRAMICOURT	Meteorological. Fine morning – rain in afternoon. Training under O.C. Sqn.	

WAR DIARY
or
INTELLIGENCE SUMMARY

(Erase heading not required.)

Army Form C. 2118.

"A" Squadron
N. Somerset Hussars

Volume VI

Hour, Date, Place	Summary of Events and Information	Remarks and references to Appendices
PM 7.0 April 21st 1916 FRAMICOURT	Meteorological Fine morning — rain commenced in afternoon - recommenced night 20/21st. Training with cyclists & M.G. Section.	Continuous heavy rain made horse lines in a very bad condition - orders to take horses on to the grass if it was not wet while so mounted.
PM 7.0 April 22nd 1916 FRAMICOURT	Meteorological Wet all day. Parade cancelled.	
PM 7.0 April 23rd 1916 FRAMICOURT	Meteorological Fine — cloudy intervals	
PM 7.0 April 24th 1916 FRAMICOURT	Meteorological Bright warm Training — Brigade Exercise - Concentration - 2 Sq/28th 15pm LHY, 2 sections MMG + 4 platoons cyclists set out to take up line covering concentration with remainder Sqdn 8A, cyclists & MMG in support while the Main body 30th Division on 27th inst. Sqn LHY received orders to rejoin 28th inst billet a night of 26th inst at HANGEST or BOURDON	
PM 7.0 April 25th 1916 FRAMICOURT	Meteorological Bright warm Training - 2nd Wiltshire Yeomanry to Arrange Cup of Division - 30th Lancers no hostile force. Sunny - V. warm	
PM 7.0 April 26th 1916 HANGEST-sur-SOMME	Meteorological Sqn marched out at 9.0 AM arrived 2.45 PM Midday halt 15 hrs at AIRAINES good water obtained Operation order No 13 received from 30th Bn on arrival at billets for night — acknowledged	Same billets no sewing to FRAMICOURT No sore backs but a considerable number of horses knocking HHS

WAR DIARY
or
INTELLIGENCE SUMMARY

(Erase heading not required.)

Army Form C. 2118.

Instructions regarding War Diaries and Intelligence Summaries are contained in F. S. Regs., Part II, and the Staff Manual respectively. Title pages will be prepared in manuscript.

Hour, Date, Place	Summary of Events and Information	Remarks and references to Appendices
7.0 PM April 27th BREILLY CHATEAU	Meteorological Sunny & V. warm — Left 9.0 AM arrived 10.45 AM — V. dusty on road —	Billets at Chateau Same as previous
7.0 April 28th BREILLY CHATEAU	Meteorological Sunny & warm — Training — not reading Aitchison classes etc.	Staff Horses. 2 Packhorses arrived for Aitchison first time.
7.0 April 29th BREILLY CHATEAU	Meteorological Sunny & warm — Training as above	Health of men during month Good.
7.0 April 30th BREILLY CHATEAU	Meteorological Sunny & V. warm	

J.H. Crombie Major
OC

War Diary
A. Sqn.
1/ Lancs Hussars
30th Arc. Car. Sqn.

www.ingramcontent.com/pod-product-compliance
Lightning Source LLC
Chambersburg PA
CBHW081457160426
43193CB00013B/2512